LET'S FIND OUT! OUR DYNAMIC EARTH

# THE ROCK CYCLE



SARA HOWELL

Britannica Educational Publishing
IN ASSOCIATION WITH
ROSEN
EDUCATIONAL SERVICES

*For Charlotte*

Published in 2018 by Britannica Educational Publishing (a trademark of Encyclopædia Britannica, Inc.) in association with The Rosen Publishing Group, Inc.
29 East 21st Street, New York, NY 10010



Distributed exclusively by Rosen Publishing.
To see additional Britannica Educational Publishing titles, go to rosenpublishing.com.

First Edition

**Britannica Educational Publishing**
J.E. Luebering: Executive Director, Core Editorial
Mary Rose McCudden: Editor, Britannica Student Encyclopedia

**Rosen Publishing**
Amelie von Zumbusch: Editor
Nelson Sá: Art Director
Nicole Russo-Duca: Designer & Book Layout
Cindy Reiman: Photography Manager
Ellina Litmanovich: Photo Researcher

**Library of Congress Cataloging-in-Publication Data**

Names: Howell, Sara, author.
Title: The rock cycle / Sara Howell.
Description: New York: Britannica Educational Publishing, in Association with Rosen Educational Services, 2018. | Series: Let's find out! Our dynamic earth | Audience: Grades 1–4. | Includes bibliographical references and index.
Identifiers: LCCN 2017019542| ISBN 9781680488302 (library bound : alk. paper) | ISBN 9781680488296 (pbk. : alk. paper) | ISBN 9781538300282 (6 pack : alk. paper)
Subjects: LCSH: Petrology—Juvenile literature. | Geochemical cycles—Juvenile literature.
Classification: LCC QE432.2 .H69 2018 | DDC 552—dc23
LC record available at https://lccn.loc.gov/2017019542

*Manufactured in the United States of America*

**Photo credits**: Cover Nerdist72/Shutterstock.com; p. 4 Leah-Anne Thompson/Shutterstock.com; p. 5 Michael Quinn/National Park Service; pp. 6, 7, 10, 13, 18, 24 © Encyclopædia Britannica; p. 8 ArtOfPhotos/Shutterstock.com; p. 9 Joel Arem/Science Source/Getty Images; p. 11 Marble zone/Shutterstock.com; p. 12 Willyam Bradberry/Shutterstock.com; p. 14 Myotis/Shutterstock.com; p. 15 © Tyler Boyes/Fotolia; p. 16 © D. L. Weide; p. 17 © Kirkendall/Spring; p. 19 Courtesy of Ernst ten Haaf; p. 20 Z. Radovan, Jerusalem; p. 21 Arndale/Shutterstock.com; p. 22 Glen Allison/Getty Images; p. 23 BGSmith/Shutterstock.com; p. 25 Konstanze Gruber/Fotolia; p. 26 Grant Dixon/Lonely Planet Images/Getty Images; p. 27 Jane Selverstone; p. 28 Adwo/Shutterstock.com; p. 29 JGI/Jamie Grill/Blend Images/Getty Images; back cover and interior pages background © iStockphoto.com/vicsa.

# Contents

# A Rocky History

Millions of years ago, Earth looked very different than it does today. Over time, rocks have been formed, worn down, and formed again. This is called the rock cycle. A cycle is a series of events or actions that repeat regularly. There are several cycles in nature. The seasons are a cycle. The way water moves around Earth is called the water cycle.

Scientists can find clues to Earth's past by studying how its rocks have changed or moved. For example, rocks

**Though rocks seem to be an unchanging and permanent part of Earth, they are actually part of an endless cycle of change.**

Traces of extinct sea creatures, such as this trilobite, are a sign that land was once underwater.

can show us that large areas of land were once covered by thick layers of ice. Layers of rock can show us how ancient earthquakes shaped mountains and valleys. The tiny **fossils** of ocean creatures found in rocks can show us how some areas that are now dry land were once covered by water. In fact, the history of Earth can be told in rocks!

**Vocabulary**

**Fossils** are the remains or traces of plants and animals that lived long ago.

# What Are Rocks?

Rock, or stone, is a hard material made up of one or more minerals. Minerals are inorganic substances, meaning that they do not come from an animal or a plant. Rock makes up the outer layer of Earth, called the crust. At its thickest, the crust is about 19 miles (31 kilometers) thick. The lower parts of this layer

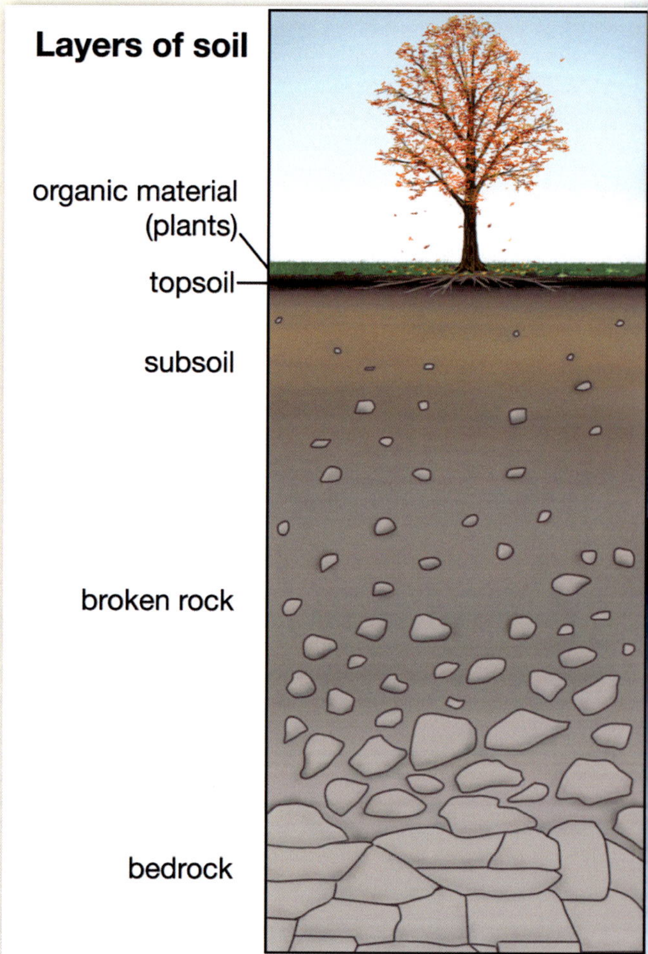



**Soil is made up of topsoil, subsoil, and broken rock. Beneath is solid bedrock.**

The sedimentary rock shale forms in muddy lagoons, floodplains, and similar areas.

are solid rock, or bedrock. Broken bits of rock lie on top. The tiniest bits of rock make up sand and soil. Underneath Earth's crust is another layer of mostly solid rock, called the mantle. Pools of melted rock, or magma, form in the upper part of the mantle and the lower part of the crust.

Scientists divide rock into three main types. These are igneous, sedimentary, and metamorphic rock. Each of these types of rock forms in a different way.

**Compare and Contrast**

**What do the mantle and crust share in common? In what ways are they different?**

# MINERALS

Minerals make up Earth's rocks, sands, and soils. They are found on Earth's surface as well as deep underground.

Mineralogists, or people who study minerals, have identified hundreds of minerals. Some of the most common minerals are metals—for example, gold, silver, copper, and platinum. Diamond, quartz, sulfur, mica, talc, and salt are other well-known minerals.

Mineralogists use certain properties to identify minerals: color, luster, hardness, cleavage, and streak.

**VOCABULARY**

**Luster** describes how a mineral appears as it reflects light. Some minerals are transparent, or see-through. Others are iridescent, which means that their color changes as light hits them from different directions.

**The mineral quartz is made up of silicon and oxygen atoms.**

**A mineral's streak is not always the same as its body color. Black hematite, seen here on the left, has a red streak.**

Cleavage is how minerals split or break. Streak is the color a mineral leaves when rubbed against rough porcelain. Mineralogists also use other tests, including how the mineral reacts to electricity or magnets.

Most rocks contain several types of minerals. For example, the rock granite is largely composed of the minerals quartz, feldspar, and mica.

# CHANGING ROCKS

Temperature, pressure, and changes in conditions at and beneath Earth's surface drive the rock cycle. The cycle consists of several natural processes that form, break down, change, and reform rocks over time.

The process of weathering wears rocks down, while the erosion process carries away weathered bits of rock. Over millions of years these bits of rock build up, harden, and become solid sedimentary rock. If that rock becomes deeply buried, it may melt into

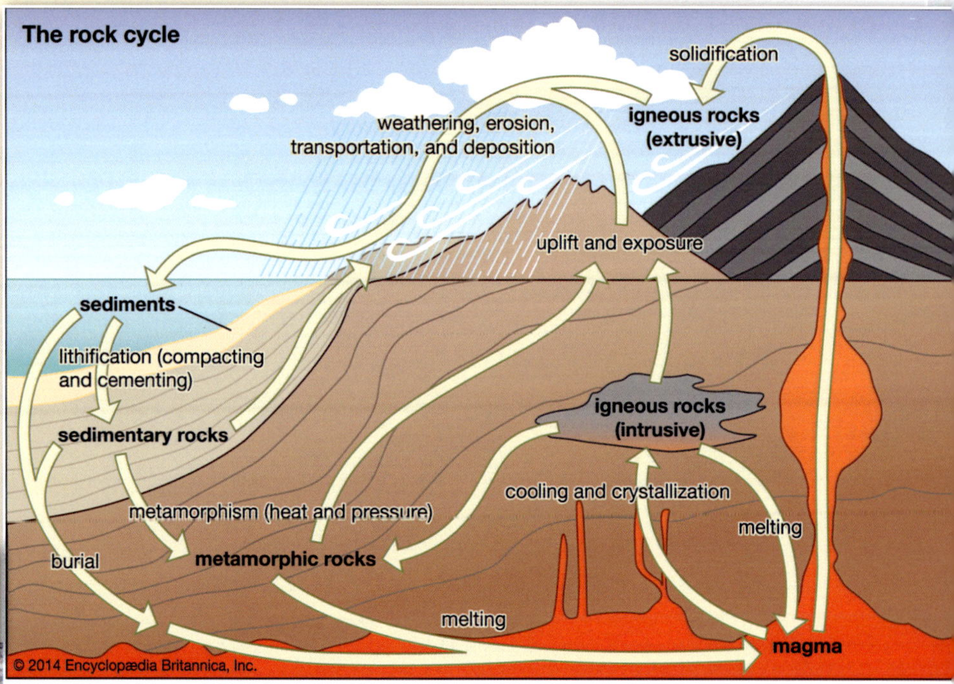


**Over millions of years, the rock cycle slowly builds, breaks down, and alters the rocks in Earth's crust.**

**Marble is a type of metamorphic rock that used to be a sedimentary rock called limestone.**

magma. When magma cools down, it becomes igneous rock. Heat and pressure inside Earth's crust can shape old rock into metamorphic rock.

The rock cycle takes many millions of years, and rocks can follow many paths through the cycle. Any of the three types of rock can change to any other type of rock under the right conditions.

### Compare and Contrast

**How is sedimentary rock similar to igneous and metamorphic rock? In what ways is it different?**

# Igneous Rock

The word "igneous" comes from *ignis*, which is the Latin word for "fire." Igneous rocks got their name because the magma from which they form is so hot. Magma is a soft, fluidlike substance. It is formed inside Earth, where the temperatures are very hot. Magma exists at temperatures of 1,100° to 2,400° F (600° to 1,300° C).

Magma is less dense than the surrounding solid rocks, so it rises toward the surface. It may settle within the crust or erupt at the surface

**Volcanic eruptions may be destructive. However, the lava they spew out eventually hardens into igneous rock.**

obsidian porphyry



**Obsidian and porphyry are just two of the many kinds of igneous rocks.**

**VOCABULARY**

**After magma breaks through Earth's crust, it becomes known as lava.**

from a volcano. If it erupts it becomes a lava flow. When magma cools down, it returns to a solid state and become igneous rock.

Most of Earth's crust is made up of igneous rock. Examples of this type of rock include granite, basalt, and obsidian.

The color of granite varies based on the different minerals that it contains.

There are two main types of igneous rock. They are called intrusive and extrusive rock.

Intrusive igneous rock forms when the magma cools slowly, usually deep underground. Granite is an intrusive igneous rock.

**Think About It**

The most common igneous rock on Earth is basalt. Why do you think that is?

**Obsidian is a glassy igneous rock formed by the rapid cooling of lava. It has long been used as a natural material for weapons, tools, and ornaments.**

Extrusive igneous rock forms when magma cools very quickly. This tends to happen when it erupts from a volcano as lava. The air and water above ground are much cooler than the lava. Basalt is an example of this type of rock. Some extrusive rock is formed from pieces of debris that are thrown out of a volcano during an eruption. If there are no minerals present, the rocks are glassy, such as in obsidian.

# CRYSTALS

Granite can be a coarse- or medium-grained igneous rock. It is rich in quartz and feldspar.

Most igneous rocks are made of crystals. In science, a crystal is a certain type of solid object. Scientists describe matter, or everything that can be seen, according to the way it is made. All matter is made up of tiny parts called atoms and molecules. If those parts are arranged in a regular pattern, then the object is a crystal. On the outside, crystals have a regular pattern of flat surfaces that meet in sharp corners.

Magma usually forms crystals when it cools. As intrusive rock cools slowly, it has time to form large crystals.

Basalt sometimes forms columns. This columnar basalt is at Devils Postpile National Monument in California.

This results in coarse- or medium-grained rocks.

When extrusive igneous rock is formed, the lava cools so quickly that crystals have little or no chance to grow. The rocks that form may be fine-grained, with minerals so small that they cannot be seen without a microscope.

### Compare and Contrast

How are intrusive and extrusive igneous rocks similar? How are they different?

# SEDIMENTARY ROCK

Calico Rock sandstone

shell limestone



Sedimentary rock can be formed in several ways. Some is formed through erosion. This happens when rocks of any kind are worn away by rain, wind, and other elements. Tiny fragments of the original rock, along with dissolved minerals, are carried away to another site. There, they may combine with other materials, such as mud. This settled matter is called sediment.

As layers of sediment build up over thousands of years, they are

**Calico rock sandstone (also called laminated sandstone) and shell limestone are two kinds of sedimentary rocks.**

Formed about four million years ago, this rock is called Old Red Sandstone.

## Think About It

Can you guess what size fragments the rocks called sandstones and mudstones contain?

compressed, or squashed, and become bonded together. Sometimes the fragments are too big to be compressed. In that case, the spaces between the fragments are filled in by the dissolved minerals, which make a kind of cement when they harden.

Sedimentary rocks can be put into groups according to the way they are created and the size of the fragments that they contain. For example, conglomerates are made of larger particles with minerals between them acting as cement to hold them together.

Another kind of sedimentary rock forms in shallow bodies of water. When the surrounding air is very dry, the water may evaporate, or dry up, leaving behind minerals that harden into rock.

Sedimentary rock can also form when the shells of sea creatures fall to the floor of the sea after the creatures die. When the shells form a thick enough layer, they become compressed and form rock. This is called limestone. Limestone is used to make cement, roads, and fertilizer. Many forms of limestone are used as building materials. People use limestone for making floors,

**The Dead Sea is actually a very salty lake in southwestern Asia. Rock salt forms along its shore.**

Limestone is found all over the world. The famous white cliffs of Dover, in England, are made up of a soft form of limestone called chalk.

for covering the walls of buildings, and for making monuments. Limestone is useful for building because it does not easily wear away and it is not difficult to shape. Over time, limestone buildings and monuments turn from white to gray.

### Think About It

Many limestone deposits contain fossils. How might limestone help scientists learn more about the planet's development?

# LAYERS

One interesting thing about sedimentary rock is the fact that it forms in layers. Each layer may have a different color, particle size, or type of cement.

Scientists study these layers. They can figure out what kind of sediment each layer is made from, as well as how it was carried to the spot where it hardened into rock. The deepest layers are the oldest. More recent layers are closer to the surface. Each layer contains unique types of rocks and

**The different colored layers of sedimentary rock can be clearly seen in these mountains.**

**VOCABULARY**

**Fossil fuels** are the remains of organisms that lived long ago. People use fossil fuels to make electricity, heat homes, and power machines.

fossils. These give scientists many clues about Earth's history.

Layers of sedimentary rock are also important because they contain important natural resources, such as salt deposits and groundwater. The world's store of fossil fuels (oil, natural gas, and coal) is also buried in sedimentary rock.

Sedimentary rock sometimes contains fossils. This sandstone has the remains of a turtle.

# METAMORPHIC ROCK

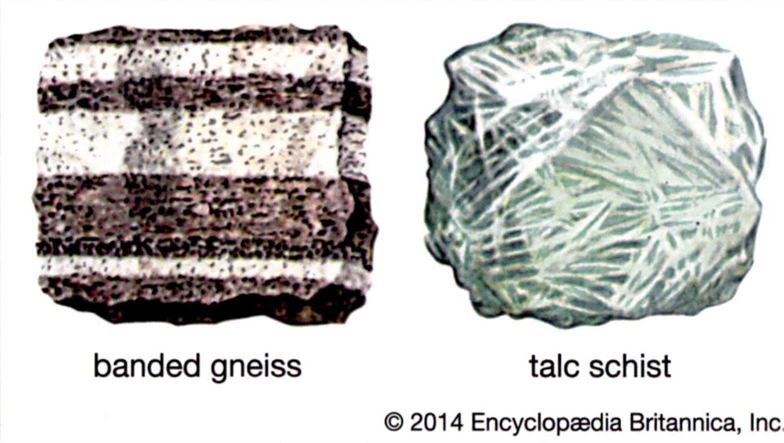


**Banded gneiss and talc schist are metamorphic rocks. One has more distinct bands than the other.**

The third type of rock found on Earth is metamorphic rock. The name *metamorphic* comes from Greek words meaning "change of form."

Metamorphic rocks are made when other rocks are affected by great temperatures and pressures. These rocks do not melt, but they do form new minerals, textures, and crystal structures. Sometimes, the minerals get separated into visible bands.

## Compare and Contrast

**How are the bands in metamorphic rock like the layers in sedimentary rock? How are they different?**

Metamorphic rock can form from igneous rock, sedimentary rock, or another metamorphic rock. The most common metamorphic rock is perhaps gneiss (pronounced "nice"), which can form from granite under intense temperatures and pressures. Marble and slate are two more examples of metamorphic rocks.

Studying the chemicals that make up metamorphic rock can reveal the original rock type. The sedimentary rock limestone can become marble. Limestone and marble are both made of calcium carbonate.

**Different minerals or different crystal sizes of the same minerals caused the bands in this gneiss to form.**

Metamorphic rock often forms in places where large sections of Earth's crust called plates come together and push against each other. When two plates collide, great temperatures and pressures can be produced. Such plate collisions can cause new mountain ranges to form. Most of the world's mountain belts are at least partly made of metamorphic rocks. Spectacular examples are provided by the Highlands of Scotland, the Alps in Europe, the Himalayas in Asia, and the northern Appalachians in North America.

**This schist rock outcrop is found in the Southern Alps, a mountain range in New Zealand.**

Greenschist is a metamorphic rock. It forms from the igneous rock called basalt.

Metamorphic rock can also form in places where magma is forced through existing rocks, heating them and increasing the pressure. Sometimes rocks are changed in a less dramatic way, when layers of overlying heavy rocks put huge pressure on them.

### Think About It

Metamorphic rocks most often form deep within Earth. Why do you think that is the case?

# Looking at Rocks

The study of the physical features and history of Earth is called geology. Geology is an important science for many reasons. It answers questions about how Earth came to have its present shape and form. It is useful for finding important materials in Earth's crust, such as oil. Geology is also helpful for predicting earthquakes and other natural hazards.

Scientists who work in geology are called geologists. It is thanks to them that we know about the rock cycle.

**This geologist is studying banded iron formations in Australia.**

## Think About It

**Where do you think rockhounds find rocks?**

You don't need a degree in geology to learn more about rocks, though. Collecting rocks and minerals is a popular hobby. Rock collectors call themselves rockhounds. They use a number of simple tests to help identify their finds. A magnifying glass and rock hunter's guidebook are useful, too. However you must understand the rock cycle to learn how a rock formed—or what it could someday become.

**Collecting and studying rocks is a great hobby no matter where you live.**

# Glossary

**atom** One of the tiny particles that are the building blocks of all matter.

**bedrock** The solid rock lying under surface materials (as soil) that are not in layers.

**cement** A binding element or substance.

**crust** Earth's thin, rocky outer layer.

**crystal** A solid form of a substance or mixture that has a regularly repeating internal arrangement of its atoms and often external plane faces.

**deposit** A collection of mineral matter in nature.

**evaporate** To turn from a liquid to a gas.

**fragments** Parts that are broken off.

**groundwater** Underground water that supplies wells and springs.

**mantle** The layer of Earth lying between the crust and the core.

**molecule** The smallest unit of a substance that has all the properties of that substance. Molecules are made of atoms.

**monument** A building, pillar, stone, or statue honoring a person or event.

**porcelain** A kind of pottery.

**pressure** A force that can move or press down on things.

**properties** Special qualities or features.

**soil** A mixture of minerals and organic materials that covers much of Earth's surface.

**temperature** The degree of hotness or coldness of something (such as air, water, or the body) as shown by a thermometer.

**weathering** A natural process that slowly breaks apart or changes rock.

# For More Information

## Books

Dee, Willa. *Erosion and Weathering* (Rocks: The Hard Facts). New York, NY: PowerKids Press, 2014.

Nelson, Maria. *Igneous Rocks* (That Rocks!). New York, NY Gareth Stevens Publishing, 2016.

Romaine, Garret. *Geology Lab for Kids: 52 Projects to Explore Rocks, Gems, Geodes, Crystals, Fossils, and Other Wonders of the Earth's Surface*. Beverly, MA: Quarry Books, 2018.

Tomecek, Steve. *Dirtmeister's Nitty Gritty Planet Earth: All About Rocks, Minerals, Fossils, Earthquakes, Volcanoes, & Even Dirt!* Washington, DC: National Geographic Children's Books, 2016.

Van Rose, Susanna. *Volcano & Earthquake*. New York, NY: DK Children, 2015.

## Websites

Because of the changing nature of internet links, Rosen Publishing has developed an online list of websites related to the subject of this book. This site is updated regularly. Please use this link to access the list:

http://www.rosenlinks.com/LFO/Rocks

# Index